W RDS

I AM

THANKFUL

God Has Taken Me To A Higer Place

And A Greater Dimineson To Him

SANDRA MCCOY

I AM THANKFUL by Sandra McCoy; A Personal Testimony Published by - CreateSpace, a DBA of On- Demand Publishing, LLC. 2013 and KDP/Amazon 2018.

Cover by Royalty Free Images from Colourbox

Copyright© 2018 – 1st edition - by Sandra McCoy – All rights reserved.
Library of Congress Cataloging-in-publication data:McCoy, Sandra
I am thankful / Sandra McCoy --- 1st ed. p. cm.

ISBN-10:
1719228590
ISBN-13:
978-1719228596

I AM THANKFUL
Printed in the United States of America

Also by Sandra McCoy

Declarations of Destiny
Poetry

Hearts on Fire
Love poems for married couples only

In Your Twilight
Inspirational Poetry

"Am I My Brother's Keeper?"
Play

Lord Save Our Children
Play

Ebony Shadows
1st Book of Poetry

Table of Contents

Foreword

We are honored to be able to write this foreword for "I AM THANKFUL." Sandra has written the personal testimony that creates a clear, thoughtful, and extremely readable overview on the various characteristics and names of God. In fact, she found some we did not know about.

We met Sandra fifteen (15) years ago in Highlands, California, as she walked the streets as a community organizer. We gave her a glass of water, and we have been talking ever since. We are very excited for Sandra. She is an awesome prayer warrior and intercessor.

Throughout this book, you will also see her personality woven within her writing.

Sandra reveals her humorous side as she talks about "going to hell and back with gasoline drawers on," and equates it with the scorching flames and fires of everyday life trails. Then she looks in the rearview mirror of her life and speaks about being wrapped in grave clothes as an avalanche of pain flooded her very being. You will see the inspiration that fills her. You will understand how she can light up a room when she walks in.

The twist comes as Sandra presses into God, and He leads her through the roads of hells fire. While pressing in, God reveals Himself to her in the many characteristics wrapped in His names.

He turns her mourning into dancing, gave her beauty for ashes, and speaks about how we are wonderfully and beautifully made. We feel that this is something so many people do not realize but need to know.

This whole book has touched us. It is an enthusiastic celebration of Sandra's encounter with God at different stages of her life.

"This book will encourage you." It is a must read.

Pastors Calvin/Sheree Lyons of Judah Kingdom Apostolic First Ministries now residing in Natchitoches, Louisiana.

Acknowledgements

Most importantly, I am thankful to the incredible God for fortifying me to finalize this extraordinary work.

As the author, I wish to thank several people.

I am grateful for my overseers, Pastors Jonathan and Christina Miller. I express my deepest appreciation to Pastors Calvin/Sheree Lyons for taking the time to write the foreword for, "I AM THANKFUL."

I would also like to thank my colleagues, Pastor Marty Norman, Prayer Ministry and Valerie Jenkins, who were my eyes and ears for this work. Thanks for your tremendous, required input.

I would like to express my gratitude to the many people who saw me through this book; to those who provided support, talked things over, offered comments, and assisted in the editing, proofreading and design.

Love, Sandra

Dedication

This book is dedicated to the Lord Jesus Christ who consistently downloads His creativity within me.

To my parents, Nathaniel and Frances, for without them there would be no me. Also, to the pieces of me: my sons Jay and Jamar, and my sweetheart and grandson, Keeylan.

Throughout your lives, always remember how deeply and unwaveringly I love you all.

Much love

The Making

It took me a while to get here, but I can now say that I am thankful to God for what I've been through...key words **"been through."**

It was not for the breaking but for *the making.* I thank Him for how He kept me and never left me; what He taught me and how He brought me; for leading and guiding me; providing for me and making ways out of no way for me.

The Lord has turned everything the enemy has done for evil to work for my good…just like He said He would. God caused favor to stick to me like honey, and finally the release of all my money…lol…hallelujah!!!

Anything that could be shaken couldn't stay, and all that I didn't need sent them on their way. I had to fight my way in and through places I never thought I'd be. With His grace and mercy, He kept right on loving me. He reassured me that I was safe in His arms in spite of all the spells, hexes, jinxes and charms.

All those who mocked me, criticized me on half-truths—God has made them ashamed. For all the lies, He brought truth to the forefront. All fake friends, (friend-enemies), He exposed. For reproach and disgrace, He gave me more mercy and double grace.

This has made me stronger, wiser, better…gave me momentum to keep on keeping on; keep on believing; keep on trusting His word. What He ordained, and His prophecy over me, must come to pass. Regardless of the past, obstacles, limitations, and stagnation, God's Word concerning me would not return to Him void. For all these things were for my elevation in Him even though most times it didn't feel like it.

It was strengthening me, teaching me, building me; so now I can thank all my haters, evil-doers, witches/warlocks, etc. because God used each of you to train/build me so He could use me to bring so many others out…*Glory to God.*

For such a time as this, He taught me how to pray, and none of my prayers were amiss.

He is bringing me to the forefront because now He has taught me how to fight and how to hunt.

Destiny

Destiny, destiny, destiny is calling.
The enemy stonewalling, and I was falling.

There was a burglary that happened within.
The angels came to usher me in.

In the stillness of the night,
To most I was out of sight.

Invisible and ignored when destiny knocked,
I was explored.
Then by all the people I became adored.

Everybody thought I was insane with goals.

Unreachable, since I didn't agree with their point of
views, they deemed me unteachable.

A risk taker, a destiny shaker.

On the edge, I made a pledge,
To swim upstream when most swim down.

It was God who provided the turn around.

There is no time to waiver,
It is His time of favor.

I removed the chains that bind,
Severed each one from my mind.

I had to tell it; it was out of time.

I am now on God's dime.

I unlocked the shackles that held me,
Colored the vile wounds that scared me.

I came through the blood of the Lamb.
I was stamped approved by the Great "I AM."

To those who said it couldn't be done,
It wouldn't be done…
Through Christ, the victory has been won.

Jesus came and took me out of jail,
It was through His ransom I made bail.

I requested my recompense and awards for damages done, and it was granted by the blood of His dear Son.

God beckoned and said to me,
"Daughter, it is time for you to walk on water."

Though I had not yet emerged,
But I was on the verge.

They put up roadblocks to stop me,
And detours to block me.

Every attack of the enemy that tried to
derail me, damage me, dictate to me,
limit me, hold me, rape me, scold me,
judge me, rob me, hurt me, desert me…
No longer can you control me, beat me.

Wanted a tragic end for me,
So, you tried to curse me, vex me,
hex me, root me, kill me.

I came to tell you that it just ain't happening.

You no longer have the power to torment my very being.

My enemies came one way,
But by seven, they are fleeing.

Then they tried to blame me, desired to shame me,
Went out of their way to frame me.

The sabotage designed to hi-jack my destiny, steal my identity, and to make my accomplishments insignificant.

The pain that came to claim me.

Storms rose to drown me,
The struggles wanted to dismiss me.

Circumstances came to frustrate me, clown me.

Trials and tribulations threw me in the fiery furnace designed to burn me.

All these things could not be, because
success lies deep within me.

I didn't break down this time around,
Nor did I quit because this is it.

I flipped the script in my mind for scriptural recall.

He taught me how to fight to break down the wall.

But it was God who kept me, never left me.

He Loves me, He holds me, He taught me, He brought me, He healed me.

He provides and protects me.
He leads me, He guides me.
He delivered me, empowered me.

Jesus came and vindicated me.

God's angels walked me through an opened door.
He knew I had not passed this way before.

He told me, "Before I formed you in the belly, I knew you. Before you came forth out of your mother's womb, I sanctified you."

He ordained me a prophet to the nations,
after He completed my much-needed renovations.

To reveal God's glory through my words,
actions and deeds, I will publish the name of the Lord...
Writing and sharing the Word of God, I plant His seeds.

Day by day, hour-by-hour, I take back my power.

Go ahead and take a good look.

I am an open book.

A picture of magnificence; born to make
a difference.

A minister, a flaming fire.

Every round goes higher and higher,

and Satan is a bold-face liar.

God has made me for signs and wonders.

Through Him, I am more than a conqueror.

My future is bigger and brighter than anything in the past. He gave me a new perceptive—something that would last.

And so, I'm moving beyond the old and into the new.

I did not come to do you.

Walked out of the past, into my present,

and soared into my future.

Moved far beyond and into elevation, illumination,

activation, determination, perpetual favor,

and continuous adaptation.

From faith to faith, and glory to glory,

God rewrote my story.

This land that I am now possessing,

God has opened the windows of blessing.

No longer absent, but now a militant—as the heavens

suffer violence, and the violent take it by force.

I am the violent…I will run the race

and complete the course.

I will not defer; I will not concede; I will keep it moving.

I arose, for my light had come, and the glory of the Lord has risen upon me.

To be all He created me to be.

Everything has changed,
and I have been released to reign.

By Sandra McCoy © 2013 & 2018

Scripture: Psalm 100:4

"Enter His gates with thanksgiving and enter into His courts with praise; be thankful unto Him and bless His name."

A Personal Testimony

I love this quote by Joseph Campbell…

"In the cave you fear to enter lies the treasure you seek. As each one of us continue to embark on the journey that is life, we will face challenges that will test us, defeat us, and transform us; however, we will only find that out when we courageously take the first step into the cave of the unknown."

I Am Thankful

Now I can truly say that I am honored.

Jehovah Yahweh, the Lord God, choose me to go through the things that I went through—lies, accusations, separation, divorce, joblessness, rejection, poverty, sabotage, child custody battle, scandal, deception, gossip, and more—being made so low that only God could raise me up. I walked through so much that I had to inquire of the truth from the Lord so that I could tell it to myself. He reminded me: "To who much is given, much is required" (Lk 12:48). God taught me to endure hardness as a solider. He so graciously entrusted me with those battles but gave me victory so that I could inspire and encourage you.

It is no secret that I've been to hell and back with gasoline drawers on so that I could share with you today, not only by words but experience. I agree where scripture says: "When thou walkest through the fire, thou shalt not be burnt; neither shall the flame kindle upon thee" (Isa 43:2). Painful experiences are equated to fire and flames. In light of how the very troublesome and extremely heinous trials are to every aspect of our beings, those things are as gold and silver in the fiery furnace trying God's grace upon my life as I navigated the difficult times. Even so, I know the saints are not destroyed by them. We lose nothing but their dross (the residue of things past); our standards and callings are tested, and they are reinforced through it all which has been inexhaustibly confirmed by the Hall of Fame in Hebrews, Chapter 11 (Isaiah 43:2).

There were other martyrs of Jesus in Psalm 66:12. Scripture states: "Thou hast caused men to ride over our heads; we went through fire and water, but Thou brought us out into a wealthy place, or a large place." In other words, Jesus brought us through many dangers of every kind—those that we knew about as well as those unknown. But He brought us out into a wealthy place, a place of abundance, sustenance, and even a pick-me-up, shall I say.

After enduring all the hardships and difficulties, trials, persecutions, and tribulations as each of us journeyed through that season of our lives, because the Lord was with us, we came through as pure gold. Now, according to Isaiah 45:3, God promised that He will give you the treasures of darkness—riches stored in secret places—so that you may know that He is the LORD, the God of Israel, who summons you by name. This is true. Oh, glory to God. Remember—everyone will not be happy that it's your time of harvest and blessings, but that's *their* issue. Just pray for them and keep it moving. Never, ever, ever stop moving forward.

I've learned that as you go through the scorching fires of change, you are eliminating relationships and people that need to leave your life in order for you to move forward: the dream killers, backstabbers, confusion makers, liars, etc.

Being free of the proverbial garbage cost something. When you were invited to dinner, it was free; but the chicken or cow paid the price. A price or a sacrifice always has to be made by someone or something whenever anyone or anything is made free.

I have paid the price to make other people feel comfortable and happy. I have paid the price in helping others further their careers. I have paid the price by staying in that mess of a relationship to long. Even paid the price for my loved ones each time I prayed or acted on their behalf.

While paying the price, I emptied myself. But now, through it all, I am thankful to be free and in control of my own life (with God's guidance). I am happy, alive, excited and exhilarated. It is awesome to feel physical, intellectual, emotional, spiritual and financial freedom. This can only be found in the Word of God. John 8:32 says: "…and Ye shall know the truth, and the truth (that you know) shall make you free." Absolutely *nobody* will take that from me.

I share with you today the God of many chances—the God of the turnaround. He is alive and He lives within me. I found Him to be everything I needed in any situation.

He is Baal-Perazim—the God of the breakthrough; Jehovah Nissi—the Lord is my Banner. The victory is real, and He brought me out. There is a difference in getting out and being pushed out.

As I looked in the rearview mirror, I saw a bad time that I went through in my life where I could not function at the level God created for me. I was disillusioned and disappointed. For years I ate at the table of sorrow, hurt and pain. My soul was grieving…broken in spirit, soul, mind, and dreams as the lies and gossip continued to fill the atmosphere. I was wrapped in grave clothes; an avalanche of pain flooded my very being. I couldn't find my way out and couldn't pray my way through. I felt as though all access had been denied to the throne room of grace.

I finally realized this was a weapon from the pit of hell. Satan desired to use it to steal my identity and rob me of my destiny and all God created me to be. He didn't care whom he used, or how he used them, as long as they allowed him to use them. It is amazing how folks can hate each other with a passion but will somehow come together to destroy you. However, you are a danger to the kingdom of hell when you have nothing to lose or prove.

The more I pressed into God, He loved, led, and guided me through the road of hell's fire. He turned my mourning into dancing and gave me beauty for ashes. I am thankful.

This test was not just for me but became a testimony, a catalyst of change for others walking that same road that I once traveled.

You see, He turned all those challenges to better choices—

opposition to opportunity. God gave me triple for my trials and transformed my tribulationsto triumphs. For the false witnesses that rose up against me, God brought fulfillment, as the truth always comes marching in. It may take longer than you would want but believe you me…truth will always prevail. Hallelujah!!!

He gave me happiness instead of hardship, sufficiency for shortage, and the weapon of destruction that was formed to destroy my children and me. Through prayer, it had to destroy itself; it just could not prosper. For the witchcraft and sorcery used against me, God gave me the Root of David (Rev 22:16; Psalm 64; Lev 19:31; Ex 22:18).

After I was introduced to Jehovah Rapha, the God that heals, He stopped the bleeding—the hemorrhaging—in my life, emotions, mind, spirit, soul, body, children, dreams, finances, and relationships.

I felt like Elijah when the whirlwind came. The enemy tried to take my mind, but God gave it back to me. He took the hole in my heart and gave me wholeness—nothing missing, nothing broken, and nothing lacking. Of course, I had to keep my end of the commitment and work the Word of God. It is life, and He is a God of many chances—a God of turnaround—and He has allowed me to walk in the destiny He created for me.

The unsettled matters of the heart…fears, doubt, worry,

stress, anxiety...etc. The God of compassion wiped my tears, silenced my fears, and gave me the courage to walk through the conflict. He bore stripes to usher me into my wealthy place—the place of well-being spiritually, physically, mentally, emotionally, relationally, and financially.

While living paycheck to paycheck—days, weeks and months with no check—and moving from pillow to post, God said that He would strengthen, establish and settle me (1 Peter 5:10 KJV). It was that same God who said He would supply all my needs according to His riches in glory by Christ Jesus (Philippians 4:19 KJV), and He did just that.

I can't say that it was always easy—can't say it was always comfortable—but I can say that He was, and is, always faithful.

They tried to hold up my money, checks etc....and hoped it was going to hurt me or stop me. But I didn't miss any meals. Lights still on, still got a roof over my head. They can't do anything—not one thing—unless God allows them to.

Just like with Job when God said, "Have you tried my servant, Job?" He said, "Have you tried my servant, Sandra?" So count it not strange the fiery trial which is to try you as though some strange thing happened unto you (1 Peter 4:12 KJV), but the more fiery trials you go through, the more valuable you become. The more suffering you endure, the greater your harvest, blessing and results. In the end,

Job had twice as much than he did at the beginning (Job 1:8 KJV).

As previously stated, "They can't do anything unless God allows them to." So, they don't have ANY right or authority. All they did or are doing is letting you know whose you are and who your God is. You must realize that they have a set time and must release it anyhow. The Word of God says whatever God has for you shall come to you (John 6:37).

The enemy is powerless; if he could stop you, he would have already done so. They cannot stop or block anything. You, they, them and those are just another character on a page in my book. When they (enemies) reared up at me, I said thank you 'cause I didn't know that part of me was dead. So now, I knew that I'd gone to another level by the mere fact that they still got their teeth that they were lying through…lol…Hallelujah! (Tell the truth and shame the devil…lol.) I can't be mad at them; they do not even know why they are doing this—they don't even understand.

I speak this truth in the authority given to me. If only they knew who you are in Christ, they would not have even wasted their time; if they knew that behind the scenes, God is using them on my/your behalf. If they knew that all they were doing was helping to transport you into your destiny, taking you to the next step of your purpose. If they knew that, they were the catalyst to God multiplying the gifts and talents within you to use as a vehicle to your success, they'd not only be mad at themselves but slap themselves as well.

Even though they tried so hard to abuse you financially and use you, now you're in a place to put your foot on them—but you don't, because God said, "Vengeance is mine and I will repay" (Duet 32:35). They were just a buffer for God to use to perfect, establish, and settle you.

Child of God, go ahead and close that chapter; keep walking, keep moving. People are waiting on the other side of your obedience…the other side of your breakthrough.

After God had ministered this to me, it bore witness in my spirit and it changed my focus—my point of view—on how I saw things. Literally, it was like turning my head to the right and back, a much-needed adjustment.

As you well know, you can't fix the past; only God can do that. So, refuse to be a prisoner of your past. Choose to live in the present and move toward your future. Only you can let go of the unforgiveness, bitterness, offenses, etc. Maintain that you will not be held on the level they see you or wish to hold you in. Ask God to deliver you and them. Let God be God, and no one else.

No one else has the authority to dictate your life. Determine it will not spiral down to soothe anyone insecurities. Decree that your life will only take flight and SOAR…Refuse to let folks project their will or persona on you. Do not give your power, access, or freedom for anyone else to lord over you or put you in a box.

The enemy wants to interrogate you because of the destination God has for you doesn't line up with that which he has for you. Stay in agreement with God's Word. Do not compromise your future; stand your ground and stay in faith. Be firm and stop allowing the enemy to hi-jack your life. Decide to no longer be the victim. Dump the garbage and negativity from your brain, mind, thought-life, imagination, dreams, emotions and heart.

They are not paying you rent to stay there.

Forbid the enemy to invade your mind and emotions. Don't allow the vicious cycles in life from acertain group of people to violate or impact your life negatively. The lonely, the vindictive, and the jealous at heart will hold you, try you, and pronounce you guilty as charged, but God will vindicate you.

Now I can represent Him, as I have suffered with Him. I am a life jacket for someone else. I can reach back and grab someone's mind, heart or soul, then pull them up out of their stupor, circumstance, situation, and depression so that they can find His desire for their lives. Out of that oppression comes opulence, and influence. Most importantly, shave years off their journey. Why go through the wilderness for 40 years when you can make the journey in 40 days?

The Lord held my hand and saw me through so much more than I could have ever imagined. I came to know Him as

Jehovah Shammah, the ever-present God. I am a witness that God is a very present help (Eze 1 Sam 4:1) in time of trouble no matter what it may be. Immanuel, God with us, kept me. I found solace in knowing that God (El Roi) saw and sees everything that happens and heard and hears everything that is/was said or thought (Gen 16:11-14). Sometimes we look for love in all the wrong places, but God *is* love.

On this journey, I got to know the God of peace, Jehovah Shalom (Judges 6:20-24). He gives you the peace that surpasses all understanding. Shalom also means prosperity and safety. He will have you laughing at situations in the natural that you should be crying about; making folk think that there is something wrong with you or at best that you just "crazy," because they can't see it. "If they ever had the Prince of Peace speak to a storm in their lives, they would know that in the eye of a storm walks Jesus." Need I say more (Matt 14:24-25)?

God takes the challenges and create change; He uses the obstacles to make you and over comer. In adversity, He said that I am the apple of His eye (Zech 2:8, Ps 17:8). Through all the ridicule, He fashioned me a royal diadem in the palm of His hand (Isaiah 62:3). To God be the glory, for the things He has done. Through the gossip, slander and sabotage, God requires restitution be made that whoever (burns shocks of grain) becomes a hindrance, or curse to one's neighbor, or started the (fire) gossip and slander shall surely make restitution (Ex 22:6).

He also said that as I walk through the ambushes, plots, snares, plans, traps, strategies, tactics and ploys the enemy has devised; that He would send angles before me to make the crooked places straight and the rough places smooth (Isa. 45:2). God took my sorrow and gave me success and business with a balance. Thank you, Jesus. (Isa 45:2).

In my weakness, God makes me strong.

Jehovah Sabaoth—the Lord of Host, the Lord of armies. Jehovah Gibbor is the God who defends/the Man of War. Jehovah Gibbor stands in all of His glory and splendor, and He defends me.

Blessed is the LORD my strength, which teaches my hands to war and my fingers to fight (Ps 144:1, 18:34). He taught me the art of warfare. He equipped me to become an expert in war and all weapons of war. I am a dangerous weapon strategically planted in the hand of my God. I am a solider, and I do not have to be pumped up, primed or pushed. Like stealth, you won't even see me coming. I will not break rank. He taught me how to speak His Word in authority—to speak the positive, which is in faith, in the face of fear, which is doubt and negativity. To stand on His Word after I have done all to stand, just stand (Eph 6:13). God's Word is life. His Word is Truth (John 17:17).

Pushing back against the enemy...I sling my weapons of

praise that causes my enemies to be confounded, confused, and destroy themselves (2Chron 20:22). I am a strategic sniper as I fire my weapon of prayer; it changes the outcome.

I took Him at His Word when He said, "Fear not, daughter, for I am your shield and your exceeding great reward" (Gen 15:1). God promised to defend me and bless me, so I don't have to fear the enemy's revenge or retaliation. God has got my back. Jehovah Nissi is my Banner and Victory (Ex 11:5, 17:8-16). Jehovah Jireh has continuously provided for me through famine, drought, and all the desert experiences in my life. It is El Shaddai, the God that supplies, who upgraded my standard of living.

Jehovah Rohi is the Lord My Shepard, and I shall not want for any good or beneficial thing. He prepares a table before me in the very presence of my enemies.God broke the back of poverty and granted me prosperity through tithing, offering, paying vows, and first fruit.

I have tasted and treaded the bitter waters of Mara, but the "Tree of Life," made it sweet. Oh, taste and see that the Lord is good. Just as fire refines silver, so do trails refine our character, gives us discipline and increase discernment. It ushered me into a new and deeper depth in Him (Psalm 34:8).

In the "I AM That I AM," the eternal power and unchanging

character of God; the Lord Adonai, my Lord/Master over all that I am and do—in fact, every area of my life. In Him, I found security and stability. He is trustworthy. God is the Faithful Promise Keeper. He is the God that cannot lie, and the God that will not fail. The covenant keeping God.

Father, I just want to take the time to say that I thank You. I love You, bless and appreciate all that You've done and are yet doing. I really reverence who You are in my life.

Thank You, Lord, for giving me unconditional love for rejection, teaching me to love myself and know my identity (who I am and whose I am in Christ Jesus). After all, Elohim created me in His image with His likeness. I am a vision of beauty inside and out.

"I am fearfully and wonderfully made." If Satan can steal your identity, he can steal your destiny (Psalm 139:14).

God, I thank You that everything that the enemy tried to use to break me, Lord, You used it to make me. You reached down and pulled out all the hidden treasures that You had buried in the deep crevasses of my being and gave me vision and purpose. I see the value and worth in me and can recognize the value and worth in others.

Lord, You changed my focus by giving me a new attitude and altitude, allowing me to dream out loud (bringing dreams to pass), live life to the fullest, and caused me to keep moving forward. According to the Word of God in Romans

12:2: "Do not conform to the pattern of this world but be transformed by the renewing of your mind. Then you will be able to test and approve what God's will is—His good, pleasing and perfect will." I say Amen to that.

In all that I went through, I had to remember that the "I AM That I AM" had come to deliver me out of the hands of the Egyptians—be it curses, vexes, poverty/lack, jinxes, spells, sickness/diseases, or hard times etc.—and took me across the Red Sea in my life to bring me into a good land flowing with milk and honey (the beautiful productivity of my promise land). He brought me unto the place of the Canaanites, which represents humiliation. Hittites signify intimidation and fear; Amorites embody lying and evil speaking; the Perizzites characterize division and sowing discord; the Hivites exemplify small-minded mentality, and the Jebusites denote control and domination. It was not by my might, nor by my power, but the Spirit of the Lord put them all out of my land little by little (Zech 4:6; Ex 23:30).

At this time, I didn't even realize that I was marked in the fire to carry the weight of His Glory. God let me dream yet another dream and escorted me into my destiny. So let the tongues wag and the heads roll, but don't stop; just keep it moving.

Press through the opinion of others. After all, the only thing that matters is what the Word of God says about you. So stay in agreement and speak His Word only concerning your life, children, ministry, and business etc. From the words of a famous writer, "Just keep on walking and don't look back; forget about the past, and don't look back, baby." Just keep it moving in God. Hallelujah! (Matt 8:8).

By the grace and mercy of God, I'm still here, and I am going to be here in my right mind, having the use of all my limbs, anointed, walking in health, and wealth serving my God. He is the faithful Promise Keeper, the covenant-keeping God; the God that will not lie and the God that cannot fail. Oh, glory…He did it for me, and He will do it for you— if you let Him. He is the "Amen"—it is finished.

Be Blessed, Elder Sandra

God's Not Slack Concerning His Promises

God is not slack concerning his promises. If I refuse to give in, God will surely cause me to win. Everything has shifted. God has said, "Enough is enough," and heavy burdens are lifted. My lean years are behind me, and my years of flourishing are here. The best is yet to come, and my blessing now appears.

It is my time to flourish, and my due season to thrive. The Lord has released healing into every area of our lives. Lord, you have brought me into my wealthy place. You have taken me from being overwhelmed to being overjoyed; from poverty to prosperity; pain to power; from ridicule to reigning and from trouble to testimony.

The Lord has blessed me with a blessing that cannot be reversed. Glory to God. He has covered me with His blood; dressed me in His anointing; equipped me with His power; wrapped me in His promise and smeared me with His favor.

Only You, and You alone, have given me spiritual understanding, discernment, and strategies. It is You, Father God, that have blessed me, and not me, myself. It is not by might nor by power, but by the spirit of the Lord. My life is like a dream come true. I have unprecedented favor with

God and man. Restoration is here and He has made my family one. Joy and rejoicing have increased in my life—for the joy of the Lord is my strength. The Lord has blessed me with a blessing that cannot be reversed. Glory to God. He has given me all things to enjoy. So, I am living life like it is golden. Living in full color. Living life to the fullest. I am enjoying all things now. In Jesus' name.

It is my time to see fatness on my life and walk in abundance. Because I am obedient, I will eat the good, the best, and the fat of the land. It's not over until I am running over, good measure pressed down and shaken together. I have left the valley of the shadows of death. I decree and declare that the winter season has come to an end, and flowers are now blooming and thriving in my life. Water is now flooding every dry place. My life smells like the sweetness of the Rose of Sharon. It is my time to forcefully increase.

For the heavens suffers violence and the violent take it by force. I am the violent and I take it by force. The time has come, the time is now to collect the spoils and recover all. It's my time to reap an uncommon harvest. It's my time now!!!

This is my year of fulfillment, my unequivocal time to thrive. For I am the righteousness of God, and I shall flourish like a palm tree and grow like a cedar in Lebanon. My house shall be like the house of Obed Edom; all my children and grandchildren and future generations are taught of the lord, and great is their peace. I shall still bring forth fruit in old age.

I am experiencing breakthrough after breakthrough. "I am healthy, wealthy, witty and wise. The Holy Ghost always guides me with His eyes. I am enjoying the blessing of fruitfulness and multiplication in my life. I am experiencing great increase in a short period of time.

Because the Lord my breaker goes before me, I will spend my days in prosperity and my years in pleasures. I have life and that more abundantly.

The Lord has given me my hearts' desire and some. I do not lack any good thing because the Lord has prepared a table before me in the very presence of my enemies. This is my season of great productivity and achievement, my season of elevation and promotion. New doors of opportunity are being opened, and I shall walk through.

God has spoken over my life and caused me to prosper and live-in peace. This is my season where the God of Justice rights the wrongs in my life. I thank You God that You have ordained new mercy, new grace, new prosperity, and a new beginning for my life. I now possess my promise lands. It is a good land, a land of pomegranates, and olive oil, a land of brooks, and springs.

My land flows with milk and honey.

Thank You, Father God, that Your gifts bring me prosperity. You have made me successful, and I am living in my miracle right now. Let men hear of the goodness and prosperity that you have established in my life. And I will decree that you Father God are a Great God; an Awesome God; a Sovereign, and loving God; Holy and Righteous God; a God of restoration, and recompense; a God of Justice and vindication; a longsuffering God; the Faithful Promise Keeper; the God that cannot lie; the God that will not fail. You are the God that will never break covenant…Hallelujah!

This is my year of fulfillment. He has crowned my year with His goodness. I am walking in my destiny. Be it unto me according to your Word. In Jesus name…Amen

Determine if God is Your Most High God

Establish Him as the All-Sufficient One in your life. Is He your Lord, Master, and Savior? Perhaps He is your Prince of Peace, and just possibly the Lord Who will—and has—provided for you. Is He is your Father? God knows us by our name. He knows our characteristics; shouldn't we know Him by His? He is the one and only true and living God—the Lover of our souls, the Redeemer from ourselves—and He loves us with an everlasting love.

Please see the names of God on the following pages. I believe this will help you to personalize your relationship with Him even the more. Each name reveals more of the characteristics of the Godhead.

The Names of God and Who is He in Your Circumstances

I AM THAT WHO I AM (The Covenant Keeper) Ex 3:14, John 8:57-58 Covenant Maker Gen 6:18
Jehovah – The Lord - Ex 6:2-3
Jehovah – Alpha/Omega – The Beginning/The End - Rev 21:6
Jehovah Kabodhi - The Lord, my Glory - Ps 3:3
Jehovah Ibry - The Lord God of the Hebrews - Ex 3:18
Jehovah Keren-Yishi - The Lord, The Horn of Salvation – Ps 18:2
Abba Father - Dear Father - 2 Cor 6:18; 1 Jn 3:1; Heb12:5-11
El Olam - The Everlasting/Eternal God - Gen 21:33, Ps 90:13
Jehovah Shalom - The Lord is Peace – Judges 6:20-24
El Qanna - Jealous - Ex 34:14
Jehovah/The Name of God is Yahweh – Ex 3:14; Deut 6:4; Dan 9:14

Jehovah Sabbaoth - The Lord of Hosts - Isa 1:24; Ps 46:7
Jehovah Ezer - The Lord, our Helper - 1Sam 4:1
Jehovah Jireh - The Lord will provide - Gen 22:14
Immanuel – God with us- Isa 7:14; 8:8-10; Matt 1:23
Adonai - The Lord, my great Lord - Ps 8; Isa 40:3-5; Ezek 16:8; Hab 3:19 Gen 15:2
Elohim - All Powerful, Creator of all things – Gen 1:1-3; Deut 10:17; Ps 68;Mark 13:19
El Elyon - The Most High/Sovereign God – Gen 14:18-24
Yahweh - I AM – Exodus 3:14; Mal 3:6; Deut 6:4
El Roi – The One who sees me – Gen 16:11-14; Psalm 139:7-12; Matt 22:18, 26:21, 34: Luke 5:21-24
Jehovah - "I AM," the one who is; Self-Existent One – Ex 3:14; 6:2-4; 34:5-7; Ps 102
Jehovah-Rapha – The Lord, your Healer – Ex 15:15-27; Ps 103:3; 147:3; 1 Peter 2:24

Jehovah-Rohi - The Lord, your Shepherd – Psalm 23:1-3; Isaiah 53:6; Jn 10:14-18; Heb 13:20; Rev 7:17
Jehovah-Tsidkenu – The Lord, our Righteousness – Jer23:5-6; 33:16; Ezekiel 36:26-27; 2 Corin 5:21
Jehovah-M'kadesh – The Lord, our Sanctification - Lev 20:8; Ex 19: 2-6
Jehovah Nissi - The Lord, my Banner - Ex 11:15; Ex17: 8 – 16
Jehovah Shammah - The Lord is there - Ex 48:35
Jehovah Magen - The Lord, my Shield/Buckler - Deut 33:29: Ps 28:7, 89:18
EL Shaddai – The All Sufficient One; The God of all our blessings - Gen 17:1-3; 48:3; 49:25; 35:11; Ps 90:2
Jehovah Yasha - The Lord, our Savior - 49:26
Jehovah SeL' I (She' – lah) - The Lord, my Rock - Ps 18:2
Jehovah Tsork (Tsoor) - The Lord, my Strength - Ps 19:14
Jehovah ORI (Ore) - The Lord, my Strength – Ps 27:1
Jehovah Zimrath - The Lord, my Song - Ex 15:2; Isa 12:2

Jehovah MePhaltt (Me-Paw-Lat) - The Lord, my Deliverer - Ps 18:2; 2Sam 22:3
El-Gmulot – The God of Recompense/Retribution; He will surely repay - Jer 51:56
Jehovah Yeshua – The God who saves - Ps 118:14; Lk21:30-32
Jehovah Melech'Olam - Lord King forever - Ps 10:16
Jehovah Chereb - Lord the Sword - Duet 33:29
Jehovah Elohim Israel - The Lord God of Israel -Judges 5:3
Jehovah Ez-Lami - The Lord, my Strength – Ps 28:7
Jehovah Gaal or Go'el - The Lord, Thy Redeemerkinsman – Isa 49:26, 60:16
Jehovah Gibbor - The Lord Strong and Mighty/Mighty Warrior – Isa 9:6
Baal Perazim – The God of the Breakthrough - 2 Sam5:20; Isa 28:21
Jehovah Misqab (Mis – Gawb') - The Lord, my High Tower - 2Sam 22:3; Ps 144:2
Jehovah Gibbor Milchamah - The Lord Mighty in Battle - Ps 24:8

Jehovah Matsuwd (Maw – stood) -The Lord, my Fortress - Ps 18:2
Jehovah Naheh (Naw – Kaw) The Lord Smites – Ez7:9
Jehovah GeMULAH – The Lord of Recompense –Jer 51:56
Jehovah HaMeleck - The Lord, the King - Ps 98:6
HaShem – My Name – 1 Kings 8:28-29; Ex 20:7; Ps 30:4; Philip 2:9-10
Yahweh Melek – King over every nation on earth – Ps 71:1-3
ElChay – Living God – 2Kings 19:15-16; Ps 42:1; Jer10:14
Ish – Husband – Hosea 2:16. 19-20
Jehovah Elose – God that forgave
Jehovah Avinu – Lord, our Father
God of Rehoboth – The Lord has given us room and we will flourish in the land - Gen 26:22
Jehovah Shophet – (So-phait) – Judge of the whole earth – Demands Perfect Justice – Ps 94:15, 96:1013

Eternal Rock of Ages Isa 26:4; The Word-John 1:1; The True Vine-John 15:1

A crown of glory Isa 28:5; The Spirit of Resurrection - Romans 8:11

In Isa 9:5 He is the wonderful counselor, mighty God my Father of eternity,
Prince of peace.

The Lord Himself goes before Duet – 3:18, 1:30, 1;33,31:8, Isa 45:2

The Avenger Gen 9; A witness 1Sam 12:5: God of Dreams Gen 41

The Interpreter - Gen 40; Your Redeemer Ex 6; Holy- Lev 11;44

The God of Acceleration Amos 9:13-14; God of miracles – Ex

He is compassionate, gracious, slow to anger, loving kindness, truth,
Mercy, forgiveness, and justice- Ex 24:6-7

The Cloud by day and Fire by night - Ex 13:22; Consuming Fire-Ex 27:14

The Spirit of wisdom and insight, the Spirit of counsel and might, the
Spirit of Knowledge and fear of the Lord- Isa11:2

The Chosen One – Isa 42:1; Strong and Mighty like a hailstorm – Isa 28:2

Maon, Machseh, Magen, Metsuda, Migdal-Oz:names of God are
grouped in Psalms as well as otherplaces in the Bible and mean:
Dwelling Place, Refuge, Shield, Fortress, and Strong Tower – Psalms 91

Our Law Giver – Isa 33:22; The Righteous One – Isa 53:11

The Potter – Isa 64; Echad, One, Unified – Zech14:9
Anointed One – Ps 2:2; The King of Glory- Ps 24

I will publish the name of the Lord...Psalm 9:1

The names of God was taken from
www.RosePublishing.com,
www.biblenamesofgod.com/nogtbjehovah.html and the
book Names of God and other Bible Studies.

ISBN 9781890947439, ISBN9781596362031.

"Being thankful is the key to your joy and peace. As we are thankful, the cycle of blessings is completed, and God, Himself, establishes who He is in your life or situation by showing up in one of His many characteristics."

Sandra McCoy is a native of Jacksonville, Florida now residing in Orlando. McCoy is a prayer warrior, intercessor, spoken word poet, author, playwright, poet, speaker, teacher, and minister.

McCoy's credits include being a former staff writer for the Florida Times Union and the Jacksonville Journal newspaper. She holds a master's degree in Christian Counseling, and a bachelor's degree in Mass Communications.